Bertie Wiggins' Amazing Ears

DAVID COX and ERICA JAMES

Illustrated by Pat McCarthy

OXFORD

UNIVERSITY PRESS

OXFORD
UNIVERSITY PRESS

Great Clarendon Street, Oxford OX2 6DP

Oxford University Press is a department of the University of Oxford.
It furthers the University's objective of excellence in research, scholarship,
and education by publishing worldwide in

Oxford   New York

Auckland   Cape Town   Dar es Salaam   Hong Kong   Karachi
Kuala Lumpur   Madrid   Melbourne   Mexico City   Nairobi
New Delhi   Shanghai   Taipei   Toronto

With offices in

Argentina   Austria   Brazil   Chile   Czech Republic   France   Greece
Guatemala   Hungary   Italy   Japan   Poland   Portugal   Singapore
South Korea   Switzerland   Thailand   Turkey   Ukraine   Vietnam

Oxford is a registered trade mark of Oxford University Press
in the UK and in certain other countries

Text © David Cox 1995

The moral rights of the author have been asserted

Database right Oxford University Press (maker)

First published 1995
This edition 2005

British Library Cataloguing in Publication Data
Data available

ISBN-13: 978-0-19-917976-3
ISBN-10: 0-19-917976-X

3 5 7 9 10 8 6 4

Available in packs
Stage 11 Pack of 6:
ISBN-13: 978-0-19-917973-2; ISBN-10: 0-19-917973-5
Stage 11 Class Pack:
ISBN-13: 978-0-19-917980-0; ISBN-10: 0-19-917980-8
Guided Reading Cards also available:
ISBN-13: 978-0-19-917982-4; ISBN-10: 0-19-917982-4

Cover artwork by Pat McCarthy

Printed in China by Imago

As clever as Prince Cecil

'Five times five!' said Mrs Lines.

She had a way of saying things softly
that sounded as if she was shouting
at you.

Everyone in the class wrote something
down, except Bertie.

Bertie chewed on the end of his pencil.
What was the answer? He wished he
could work it out. But he couldn't.

The trouble was, Bertie was no good at sums. No matter how hard he tried, he couldn't remember past his three times table.

He felt his ears beginning to twitch again.

Sadie Smith looked at Bertie and started to smile.

Mrs Lines looked up and said, sharply, 'Sadie! What is the matter?'

4

Sadie blushed. 'Nothing, Mrs Lines,' she said. But Mrs Lines could see for herself that Bertie's ears were wiggling. The trouble was, Bertie's ears didn't wiggle just a little bit. They wiggled and waggled as if they were waving at you.

'Bertie Wiggins!' she said. 'Stop that at once. If you spent as much time on your work as you spend twitching your ears, you'd be as clever as Prince Cecil.'

Everyone in the class grinned.
They all knew that Bertie looked
a bit like Prince Cecil.

Bertie sighed. He was fed up
with jokes about looking like a
prince.

'I hope you are all going to
watch Prince Cecil this evening,'
said Mrs Lines.

Everyone knew how clever Prince
Cecil was. Prince Cecil was very good at
sums. Prince Cecil knew his tables.

Every year the King went on
television and one of his children went
on with him. Last year it was Princess
Maude playing her trombone.

This year it was going to be Prince
Cecil saying his tables.

A huge crowd went to the royal
television show. Every year at the end,
the crowd had to clap and cheer. Then
the King made a big speech. He always
began, 'Cleverness shows in many
ways. It is most wonderful when it
shows in someone young. The royal
children...'

Every time the royal children were on television, Bertie's mum and dad would moan at Bertie. 'You may look like Prince Cecil,' they would say, 'but you'll never get on television by flapping your ears.'

That afternoon Bertie had his tea and started doing his homework. After a few minutes, he gave up and turned on the television. A lady was speaking. 'Tonight, everyone must see Prince Cecil.' Bertie turned the television off.

He went outside and sat on the doorstep. From next door he could hear music playing on the radio. Bertie began to wiggle his ears. First the left one. Then the right one. In no time at all both ears were waggling backwards and forwards in time to the music.

Mrs Green from next door came past. 'That's good, Bertie,' she cried. 'You're a real little act, you are.'

'No one else seems to think so,' grumbled Bertie.

The secret search

Just then, a car drove slowly into Bertie's street. It stopped right outside Bertie's house. A man and a woman got out. The man had a photo. To Bertie's surprise, they walked over to him.

The man looked at Bertie. Then he looked at the photo. 'It's amazing,' he said.

Bertie's mum and dad came outside. 'What's going on?' asked Mr Wiggins.

'We are from the Royal Palace,' said the woman. 'Prince Cecil has got red spots. It could be chicken pox. He can't be on the royal television show this evening. The King has ordered a secret search for a Prince Cecil look-alike.'

She pulled out a crown and put it on Bertie's head. The man held up the photo.

Mrs Wiggins gasped. 'It's our Bertie,'
she cried.

'No, it's not,' said the man. 'It's Prince
Cecil. We need your lad to take Prince
Cecil's place on the show tonight.'

Mr Wiggins opened his
mouth. Then he closed it again.
At last he said, 'On television? Our
Bertie? So we'll all be famous!'

'No you won't,' snapped the woman. 'No one will ever know. When Bertie goes on television this evening, everyone must think *he* is the prince. It's a secret you'll have to keep for ever.'

'Will we meet the King and Queen?' said Bertie's mum.

'Will there be a reward?' said Bertie's dad.

'Maybe,' said the man. 'But now we must get Bertie to the television studio.'

Bertie felt his blood run cold. Wasn't
Prince Cecil going on television to do
sums and say his tables? Bertie couldn't
even get past his three times table. And
as for sums… 'But Mum! But Dad!' said
Bertie. It was no good. Nobody would
listen.

Before Bertie could say any more, he
was in the car with his mum and dad.
They were on their way.

Bertie sat in the back of the car. He
was very worried. How could he pretend
to be Prince Cecil?

'We will go to the television studio
now,' said the woman. 'Bertie has to get
ready. And we must do something about
his ears.'

At last Bertie gasped, 'But Prince Cecil
is supposed to show how clever he is.
He's supposed to say his tables. I can't
do that!'

The woman sniffed. 'You don't have
to be clever. All the answers will be on
a screen in front of you.' She stared at
him. 'You can read, can't you?'

'Of course I can,' said Bertie.

'Good,' she went on. 'No one else
will be able to see the screen. No one
will know that you can't do your
tables.'

The King was pacing up and down in
the television studio. 'I will not wait any
longer!' he shouted. 'They must have
found someone who looks like Cecil
by now.'

At that moment, Mr and Mrs Wiggins
arrived with Bertie.

Mr Wiggins bowed. 'This is Bertie,'
he said. 'I'm glad we can help out,
Your Majesty.'

The King looked at Bertie. He smiled.
'It's amazing,' he said. 'You could be
Cecil, apart from the ears. Put Cecil's
crown on and hide your ears.'

'But Your Majesty,' said Bertie. 'I am
not Prince Cecil. I don't want to
pretend to be him.'

'Nonsense,' said the King. 'You look
like him. That's all that matters. Just do
what you're told and read what's on
the screen.'

It was time for the show to start. The people were in their seats. Bertie sat on a large chair. Music played. Then a man with a big smile spoke into the camera. 'Good evening, everyone. Tonight we are happy to welcome our young prince on the show. Prince Cecil is going to say his eight times table. What a clever lad!'

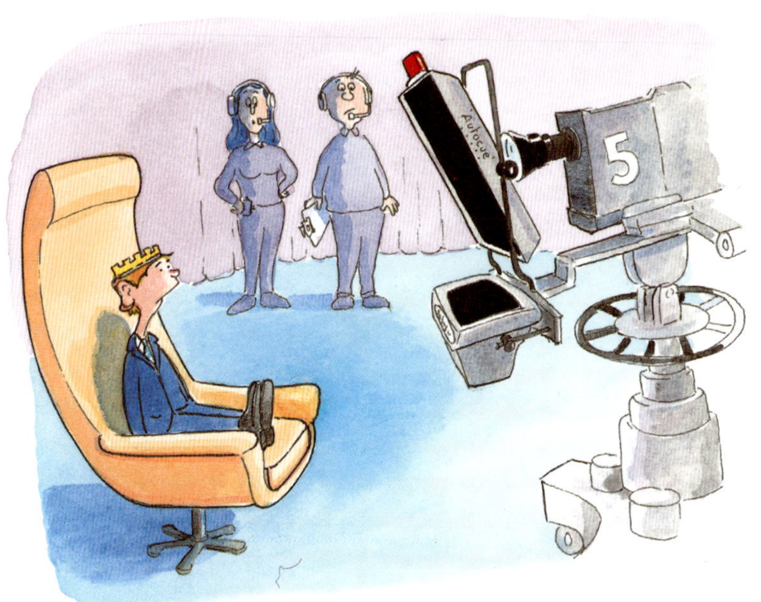

Lights shone on Bertie. A lady with headphones counted up to five on her fingers. A voice in his ear said, 'Now – ' And Bertie was on television.

Bertie felt his heart beating. He looked for the screen with the answers. There it was in front of him. He coughed, and began to read. 'One times eight is eight,' he said loudly.

Then the screen went blank.

Bertie adds it up

Bertie's tummy felt as if it had insects buzzing around inside. He wanted to be sick. He knew what came next so he gasped, 'Two times eight is sixteen.' What was three times eight?

His ears began to twitch. Prince Cecil's crown wobbled from side to side. Bertie felt the crown slip over his eyes in little jerks.

He took the crown off. This seemed to stop his ears twitching.

Then the man spoke again. He did not sound so happy now. 'Well, Prince Cecil, what are three times eight?'

Bertie tried to count the answer out on his fingers. He took off his shoes and socks and counted on his toes as well. But it was no good. He just didn't have enough fingers and toes.

One or two people called out, 'Come on! What are three times eight?' Bertie felt awful. He wanted to shout, 'I'm not Prince Cecil. I'm Bertie Wiggins.' But he couldn't say a word.

Then something strange happened. Bertie's ears began to move again. They slowly flapped back and forwards.

The crowd began to count along. 'One… two… three…' The ears flapped twenty-four times, which is exactly three times eight.

Someone shouted, 'What about four times eight?'

The ears wiggled thirty-two times.

'His ears have got it right!' cried two ladies in the front row. The crowd cheered.

By the time Bertie's ears had counted out ten times eight, the crowd were jumping up and down with excitement.

The man looked at the King. He looked at Bertie. He didn't know what to do. 'Er... Thank you, Prince Cecil... um... Or should I say, "Thanks to Prince Cecil's ears?"'

Everyone laughed, but the King scowled. 'Now the prince will do sums,' he shouted.

'Stop it, Dad!' cried a voice.

Two children darted across the studio. One was Princess Maude. The other was the real Prince Cecil. Now there were two Prince Cecils in front of the camera.

Princess Maude pointed at Bertie. 'This is not Prince Cecil,' she said.

'No, I'm Bertie Wiggins,' said Bertie.

Everyone gasped. The King went red in the face. Mrs Wiggins fainted.

Princess Maude went on, 'Prince
Cecil is not very good at sums. He hates
going on television. We both do. Last
year I had to pretend to play the
trombone. I can't really play at all.'

By now the King had jumped to his
feet. He began to roar, 'Stop the show!
Cecil! You should be in bed with spots.
Maude! Be quiet!'

But Princess Maude took no notice. 'I painted Cecil with red spots.'

'You!' cried the King.

'Yes,' said Prince Cecil. 'But we didn't think you would find someone who looks like me.'

'So we came here by taxi,' went on Princess Maude. 'We had to stop this stupid show. We hate it because it makes everyone laugh at us. They think we're too good to be true.'

The King put his head in his hands.

'But we have always gone on the royal television show. That's what it's for.'

'Yes,' said the man. He did not look happy at all. 'What about my show?'

'I know,' said Bertie bravely. 'Why don't you put on a show that children will really like? Children from all over the country could go on it.'

'Wow! Talent spotting,' said Prince
Cecil. 'What a good idea.'

'Go on, Dad,' said Princess Maude.
'Say yes.'

The King went white and then he
went red. Then he went purple. But
everyone in the studio began to clap
and cheer.

'Well… all right,' he said. 'But my
children must tell everyone what to do.'

'No, Dad,' said Prince Cecil. 'We
never want to show off again.'

'Then Bertie can do all his tables,'
boomed the King. 'And he can teach
everyone sums with his ears.'

Prince Cecil and Princess Maude
groaned.

'No sums, thank you,' said Bertie.
Then he grinned. He was enjoying
himself on television. He wiggled his
ears. 'But you wait. One day I'll really
be the star of the show.'

About the author

I was born in London in 1963, the youngest of seven children. At least twice a day I see something worth writing about.

Once I saw an elephant pushing a shopping trolley around a supermarket car park. I really did. The poor elephant had run away from a circus. I didn't know this at the time and I thought he was looking for his car. Perhaps in a story he could have been?

In case you are wondering, Erica James is not her real name. It is a pen name for a well-known children's writer.